EXIT
SMART
VOL. 2

EXIT
SMART

VOL. 2
Spotlights on Leading Exit Planning Advisors

LEADING EXIT PLANNING ADVISORS

FEATURING

Featuring:

Isaac Cohen

Mike Heckman

Stephen Cummings

Richard Dvorak

Jeffrey George

Lee Jackson

R.J. Kelly

Mark Kravietz

Michael Livian

Paul A. Kyrimis

Exit Smart Vol. 2/ Mark Imperial —1st ed.

Managing Editor/ Shannon Buritz

ISBN: 978-1-954757-25-7

Remarkable Press™

Royalties from the retail sales of **"EXIT SMART Vol 2: Spotlights on Leading Exit Planning Advisors"** are donated to the Global Autism Project:

AUTISM KNOWS **NO BORDERS;**
FORTUNATELY NEITHER DO WE.®

The Global Autism Project 501(C)3 is a nonprofit organization that provides training to local individuals in evidence-based practice for individuals with autism.

The Global Autism Project believes that every child has the ability to learn, and their potential should not be limited by geographical bounds.

The Global Autism Project seeks to eliminate the disparity in service provision seen around the world by providing high-quality training to individuals providing services in their local community. This training is made sustainable through regular training trips and contiguous remote training.

You can learn more about the Global Autism Project and make direct donations by visiting **GlobalAutismProject.org.**

CONTENTS

A Note to the Reader

Thank you for obtaining your copy of "EXIT SMART Vol. 2: Spotlights on Leading Exit Planning Advisors." This book was originally created as a series of live interviews on my business podcast; that's why it reads like a series of conversations, rather than a traditional book that talks at you.

My team and I have personally invited these professionals to share their knowledge because they have demonstrated that they are true advocates for the success of their clients and have shown their great ability to educate the public on the topic of exiting businesses.

I wanted you to feel as though the participants and I are talking with you, much like a close friend or relative, and felt that creating the material this way would make it easier for you to grasp the topics and put them to use quickly, rather than wading through hundreds of pages.

So relax, grab a pen and paper, take notes, and get ready to learn some fascinating insights from our Leading Exit Planning Advisors.

Warmest regards,

Mark Imperial
Publisher, Author, and Radio Personality

Introduction

"EXIT SMART Vol. 2: Spotlights on Leading Exit Planning Advisors" is a collaborative book series featuring leading professionals from across the country.

Remarkable Press™ would like to extend a heartfelt thank you to all participants who took the time to submit their chapter and offer their support in becoming ambassadors for this project.

100% of the royalties from this book's retail sales will be donated to the Global Autism Project. Should you want to make a direct donation, visit their website at **GlobalAutismProject.org**

ISAAC COHEN

CONVERSATION WITH ISAAC COHEN

Isaac, you are the Founder and CEO of Bedrock Wealth Strategies. Tell us about your work and the people you help.

Isaac Cohen: I'm a financial planner by trade. I decided many years ago to focus on business owners. After working primarily with baby boomers, I realized that I wanted to focus more specifically on Gen X (1964), Y, and Z business owners who don't have enough time in the day to do everything they love. I have found this group very entrepreneurial, focused on growing their businesses and their next big opportunity. I help them figure out how to get there.

Do owners know where to begin when it comes to selling a business?

Isaac Cohen: Unfortunately, not enough of them do. Every decision a business owner makes impacts the sale. Even how they set up their business at the very beginning can create significant opportunities or challenges at the sale. I have found that young entrepreneurs are very good at what they know but lack the education around some of the nuances. That's where my team and I usually come in. We help them figure out exactly what to do to prepare for sale, get time back, and increase value through value acceleration. The CPAs, CFAs, and CFPs on our team work to ensure their personal plan is squared away, freeing the owners to grow their business, sell their business, and explore their next big opportunity.

Can you give us a 10,000-foot view of your exit planning process?

Isaac Cohen: I lead the advisory team and am the quarterback of the exit planning process. I like to call myself the "cradle to grave" advisor. I typically come in early to develop the exit planning team. Often, the business is already profitable, but not always. But the business owner already sees the writing on the wall; they are just running out of time in the day, want to spend more time with family, or have found a new passion project. They often hope to sell in three or more years, but that's not a hard and steadfast rule. I focus on determining what team members need to be brought into the picture at what time so we can increase the value, figure out how to best extract the business owner, and make it more attractive for sale. When the business owner is ready to sell, not only have we already planned their personal finances, but we've planned their exit and their next steps, so they have a roadmap to get from here to there with the fewest bumps in the road.

As we are coming out of a pandemic, is it a good time to sell a business? What have you seen in your market?

Isaac Cohen: Now can still be a very good time to sell. However, we're in a very different financial environment than in 2021 and before the pandemic. To provide some reference, in the stock market today, we've seen companies with high multiples lose steam, and those growth stocks have fallen out of favor for many reasons. When growth companies get less expensive, they can become great targets for large entities with lots of capital and interest to acquire. But they also can be more selective as smaller companies find it harder to grow through lending. Investment bankers are still finding buyers for great businesses. Currently, they are looking for businesses with clear value, strong revenues, profitability, or a clear path to profitability, strong leadership, and even employee satisfaction. And frankly, the other crucial thing is the business owner can't be the most important person on the team! A buyer must see a clear path to say, "I'm ready to take the next step because this owner is leaving behind something strong when they exit."

What are some common mistakes owners make to sabotage a successful exit?

Isaac Cohen: Many business owners haven't prepared a personal financial plan. I find that business owners' personal plans and business plans are interwoven. While that can create simplicity at the onset, it also creates many complications. I urge business owners to engage planners who understand business planning and are CEPAs (Certified Exit Planning Advisors). If you plan your personal well-being first, the business sale will happen when you're ready. The key is not to let the tail wag the dog. Exit planning starts with the personal plan, leads to a business valuation, and will help inform the value acceleration process, which can drive up the sale price. The entire process can help avoid costly errors. It is also helpful to extract value from the business thoughtfully, building wealth for the owner outside of the business. Furthermore, business valuations often improve when the business relies less on the business owner. Businesses are complex, and there are so many valuable things that an exit plan can uncover. I think the biggest mistake is not to have one before you sell.

Isaac, what inspired you to get started in this field?

Isaac Cohen: My father owned many men's clothing stores throughout New York City, and growing up, I thought I would take it over one day. I really enjoyed fitting men for suits. My father didn't have an advisor or think about exiting his business when the opportunity arose. Through a series of challenges in his business and many things out of his control, his business failed. At the age of 49, he found himself unsure of what to do. Even businesses in struggling industries can sell with proper planning. I never wanted that to happen to anyone else.

*Is there anything else you would like to share
with business owners considering an exit?*

---✦---

Isaac Cohen: If you are a business owner or an entrepreneur and have thoughts like, "I'm burned out. I don't know if I can keep this up for another five or ten years," then it's time to talk to an advisor who is focused on exit planning and can bring in the right team to help get you and your business sale ready. While some great planning can be done within two years or less of the desired sale date, with a three to five-year timeframe, a business owner can do even more to save on taxes, better prepare themselves personally, and ensure that the company sells for top dollar. The business owners I advise typically have businesses valued at $10 million to $50 million. These owners usually care deeply for their employees, treat them like family, and want to ensure that everyone is benefiting. Seek out a trusted advisor who can take everyone and everything you care for into consideration.

*How can people find you, connect
with you, and learn more?*

---✦---

Isaac Cohen: www.bedrockwealthstrategies.com || icohen@bedrockwealthstrategies.com || 914-372-2878 Social Media:

Twitter handle: @Bedrock_IQ LinkedIn: Isaac Cohen CEPA, CPFA

ISAAC COHEN, CEPA, CFPA

FOUNDER AND CEO
BEDROCK WEALTH STRATEGIES

Isaac has spent more than a decade as a Wealth Management Advisor, opening his own firm Bedrock Wealth Strategies, in 2016. Isaac's area of focus includes business owners and senior employees at financial, technology, telecommunication, and cybersecurity companies. Isaac was honorably discharged from the United States Army in 2005. In his spare time, he enjoys skiing and yoga. He resides in Chappaqua, NY, with his wife Clara and their children Pamela and Gael.

He is licensed and registered to offer products and services in NY. Licenses and registrations will vary.

Domiciled in NY, CA Insurance Lic #0I10193

EMAIL:
icohen@bedrockwealthstrategies.com

PHONE:
914-372-2878

WEBSITE:
bedrockwealthstrategies.com

TWITTER:
Twitter @Bedrock_IQ

MIKE HECKMAN

Conversation with Mike Heckman

Mike, you are the founder of Sable Point Wealth Management. Tell us about your work and the people you help.

--- ⚱ ---

Mike Heckman: I think our clients are like most successful people. We work with them to relieve their financial stress. They want the freedom to do what they want to do, be with who they want to be with, and live where they want to live. They want peace of mind, free from financial worries that keep them up at night. They want to have control over their legacy, knowing they are making the maximum impact on the causes and people they care about. We see many positive impacts on business owners, retirees, and medical professionals.

How much thought do business owners
put into exit planning?

Mike Heckman: Better run businesses are easier to sell and sell for higher prices. For the people we work with, exit planning gets fully baked into their ongoing business management systems. Business owners also enjoy integrating business exit planning as a component of their personal financial planning to clarify how to maintain their lifestyle in their retirement. The Exit Planning Institute does deep research on this topic; surprisingly, 49% of business owners have not done any real exit planning or even understand what it is.

What are some pitfalls owners face if they
exit their business without a plan?

Mike Heckman: Four out of five business owners regret selling their business within twelve months of the sale. Three out of four business owners surveyed by the Exit Planning Institute *profoundly* regretted the decision. Part of this is due to improper financial integration. There may have been a lifestyle haircut they weren't expecting, and they didn't put a lot of thought into the question, "What's next?" Some of those things are within our control, and some are not. A health issue or macroeconomic event can cause businesses to shut down before the owner is ready.

In addition, many of my clients are surprised to find out how much of their personal identity was tied to the business they have grown and developed. When they leave the business, they feel lost and have difficulty determining where their personal value is coming from. So there is undoubtedly an emotional component that should be addressed.

Can you give us a 10,000-foot view of the exit planning process?

Mike Heckman: Many baby boomers who own businesses have 70 to 80% of their net worth invested directly into their business. The challenge of this significant investment in their business comes to light when there is no clear plan on who would want to buy the business or an understanding of other options to glean monetary value from the business they have built. Integrating exit planning as good business management helps determine the business's strengths, weaknesses, and opportunities. It is incredibly productive if we can help an owner envision what it would look like to get out. Do they have someone in their family who will take it over? Do they have a key employee that can step into this role? Have they considered an investment company? A lot of our work together uncovers a "business self-awareness." Then we can look at ways to improve how they run their business, calculate business valuations, and determine if they can sell the business. Some businesses are designed to close when the owner retires. These lifestyle businesses need to be integrated into the rest of their comprehensive plan for a smooth transition out of the business. Then, the who and what they care about are taken care of long after the owner leaves the business.

When is the right time to start exit planning?

Mike Heckman: The right time to start exit planning is long before you actually want to exit the business. Many business owners are surprised that proper exit planning is just a method of sound business management. When you do exit planning, it doesn't mean you will leave your business right now; it means you will have the *option* to leave your business. Every six months to a year, you should ask yourself, "Do I want to do this for another year? Or is it time to leave?" You gain control in the ability to leave your business at any time with your lifestyle planning in order. Every business is unique;

some are ready to go in six months; for others, it can be a three to five-year process.

Mike, what inspired you to get started in this field?

---⟰---

Mike Heckman: I got into financial planning mainly because my dad died when I was only 19 years old. I was the only adult son left to handle his affairs. He didn't have any estate plan set up. Going through the process, I was given a lot of good advice I didn't take and bad advice that led to some bad choices. So when I started working in an advisory role, I strived to be the financial advisor I would have wanted during that tough time with my dad. As I built relationships through growing my business, I realized that many people I served needed help in business transition planning. I reached out to the Exit Planning Institute and went through their rigorous training and testing to become a Certified Exit Planning Advisor to enable me to better serve those clients I care about.

Is there anything else you would like to share
with business owners considering an exit?

---————————⟋⟍————————---

Mike Heckman: A good plan today is better than a perfect plan tomorrow. Exit planning isn't what you think. Exit planning is the beginning of sound business management and should be done sooner rather than later.

How can people find you, connect
with you, and learn more?

---————————⟋⟍————————---

Mike Heckman: My team is ready to serve and start the process. Our website is www.sablepointwealthmanagement. com. You can also reach us by phone at 231-425-4308.

MIKE HECKMAN MS, CFP®, CEPA®

FOUNDER
SABLE POINT WEALTH MANAGEMENT

MIKE HECKMAN, MS, CFP®, CEPA®, BFA®, CDFA®, AWMA®, CRPS®, CRPC® is a nationally recognized Financial Educator, Author, Speaker, Retirement Planner, and Wealth Advisor. Mike and his team have been helping business owners, medical professionals, and retirees preserve, protect and pass on their wealth since 2009. In 2019, Mike founded Sable Point

Wealth Management, serving Western Michigan with offices in Ludington and Spring Lake. Mike is currently conducting dissertation research on wealth preservation strategies in retirement to complete his Financial Management Doctorate from California Southern University. Mike's completed education includes a Master of Science degree in Financial Planning from Kaplan University's College for Financial Planning, a BBA in Business Management from Baker College in Muskegon, MI, and he has been a CERTIFIED FINANCIAL PLANNER™ practitioner since 2014.

EMAIL:
mike@sablepointwm.com

PHONE:
(231) 425 - 4308

WEBSITE:
www.sablepointwealthmanagement.com

FACEBOOK:
https://www.facebook.com/sablepointwm/

LINKEDIN:
https://www.linkedin.com/in/mike-heckman/

STEPHEN
CUMMINGS

Conversation with Stephen Cummings

Stephen, you are the Managing Partner and CEO of Rizolve Partners Inc. ("Rizolve"). Tell us about your work and the people you help.

Stephen Cummings: Rizolve helps lower mid-market business owners, with revenues ranging from $3 to $75 million, prepare to exit their business, which in our experience, takes place over a three to five-year time frame. Many business owners are looking to retire or move on to their next act but do not know where to start. We first help them understand their objectives and goals. Secondly, we put together a plan of action. And lastly, we work alongside them on their journey through the entire process and hold them accountable to their plan goals and objectives. During that time, we help them build value, create the right picture of their company's achievements, and reach their end objectives from a valuation perspective.

How much thought do business owners put into exit planning?

Stephen Cummings: There are a couple of issues many business owners face. First, they have most likely never undertaken a disposition or sale of a company. Second, many of the team members who have helped them grow the company do not have experience executing transactions. So, there's a lack of experience and understanding about what's involved. And that's a problem. That's a problem when it comes to achieving their valuation objectives.

But there are a couple of other essential things to understand. First, they need to understand the dynamics of the market today. Many business owners, primarily baby boomers, are in the same position and looking to get liquidity on their most significant investment (many business owners have 80-90% of their personal wealth tied up in their highly illiquid business asset). So there is high supply and limited demand, which generally creates downward pressure on prices, which is a problem from an exit value standpoint. So, given the market's current dynamics, it is more essential than ever to carefully plan an exit so that the pitfalls of executing a transaction are navigated with care to protect the value created. Secondly, it is imperative to understand that they need a team of specialist advisors to chart the way forward and anticipate the issues (of which there are several) that can significantly impact value. With so many things to get done of a specialist nature, the team is bigger than just the owner!

The final point I would make is the market has several imperfections. Many services are delivered in silos across the market. This phenomenon tends to create confusion in business owners' minds as they try to develop a game plan. So having an aligned advisor team is hugely critical to creating a roadmap for the owners, affording them an element of control over the process and giving them visibility in achieving their objectives.

The core Advisory team that an owner should consider would typically comprise: a quarterback - a business Advisor like Rizolve with Exit Planning credentials and deep transaction skills and history; a Personal Financial Advisory Firm (personal and family affairs); an M&A Legal Counsel (lawyer); an accounting firm with transaction and tax planning skills (accounting and tax); and, an Investment Banker or Broker to execute the transaction (the sales team). Each set of skills should come with deep transaction experience and recent evidence of successful transaction completion to demonstrate they are knowledgeable of current market terms and conditions.

What are the common pitfalls of exiting without a plan?

Stephen Cummings: The number one pitfall is business owners need to know their magic number. They need to understand what value they absolutely need out of the transaction to fund their lifestyle goals. What do they want to do with that money? Do they want to buy a house, a yacht, a cottage, or go on a holiday? They need to know the cost. This is the role of the Personal Financial Advisory Firm - they will help you articulate your goals and then cost them for the rest of your life. Typically they would perform sensitivity analysis for changed assumptions and stress test the results for changes in macroeconomic conditions such as inflation and market returns. But the important point here is that the business owner must understand their needs and wants and that there are professionals out there that can help them define those. This underpins the sales negotiation through the transaction and creates rigidity in the bargaining position. If you know your bottom line, you know the point at which you are prepared to walk away. This sets a floor to the bargaining from the outset. This important dynamic should not be underestimated in reaching a successful conclusion between buyer and seller.

The second point is understanding the gap that the magic number creates, which is called the "value gap." The value gap is the difference between the businesses' value today versus the value the owner needs to exit the company. For example, let's say you need $5 million in cash proceeds after tax to fund your future lifestyle, but your company's value may only be $4 million today. In that example, the owner may face a value gap of $1 million. This is where Advisors become very valuable to the owner, as they can help identify and drive strategies to close the value gap in the time leading up to the transaction and help the owner eliminate the gap (or exceed the owner's goals). Understanding this equation - the difference between the actual value of the company and the owner's wants - is a key issue that needs to be worked on. In our experience, this work can take between three to five years before entering into a transaction (which will take between six to twelve months to execute on average). Many businesses fail to sell due to owners' expectations of the outcome being inflated by their own ambitions and needs.

These are a couple of crucial things a business owner needs to consider before attempting to sell their company, which need time to cure with professional help.

How has the recent pandemic affected business owners considering an exit? What have you seen in your market?

Stephen Cummings: We've seen several different scenarios with our client base. First, we've seen business owners who have been tragically hit by the pandemic and are continuing to struggle but are slowly starting to get back on their feet. The problem for these owners is that the pandemic added at least two years to their original timeframe for exiting their business because they are very weak.

The second type of situation we've seen is business owners who were hugely impacted. Still, they took the time during the two-year COVID pandemic period to invest in their business and accelerate out of the hole created by the pandemic into a better, stronger position than before. These businesses recovered quickly.

The third situation is businesses that were not affected at all, have steamed ahead, and are in better positions than ever.

It's the first situation that is the most problematic. Those business owners must understand that the timeframe is elongated into the future. If they try to sell without the proper planning extension, they will suffer a significant cut in value through the transaction. Buyers also need to see evidence of recovery; otherwise, similar cuts in valuations will likely be applied.

Stephen, what inspired you to get started in this field?

Stephen Cummings: I'm a Chartered Accountant by training with a broad background of experience in the accounting profession, global business operations, and the investment/transaction community. This is a valuable set of collective experiences. I was a CFO of a global business that was very profitable. I've also been a partner in a very large private equity firm. I got into this niche because I've "been there, done that ." I've seen many situations with young, growing companies, and I can help lower mid-market business owners along with my other partners. But the inspiration is the business owners in this particular segment and their needs. They need to get liquidity on their investment. It is typically 80% or more of their net worth, which is massive. They need it to retire and to maintain the lifestyle their family deserves. But they need to enter the shark-infested waters of a transaction in a very planned way, with full knowledge of how the market will treat them. We can help them. We have all the background to do that, including strategists, senior finance specialists, sales acceleration, marketing, and HR specialists, who were former senior executives on our team. We all work together to help business owners build value.

Is there anything else you would like to share with business owners considering an exit?

Stephen Cummings: There are two or three things that are very important to understand.

The advisor group you have worked with for many years may be able to help you through a transaction. But, as I said earlier, you need to seriously consider/review whether that group of advisors is the right group to take you through the final three years and to a successful sale. For example, a legal counsel may have served you well for many years. Still, it would be best if you had an M&A experienced legal counsel and a value growth advisor, someone like Rizolve Partners, or an accountant experienced in value growth with the time to help you throughout the year. You need a tax expert to mitigate tax exposures on a transaction and to help you plan strategic changes that will minimize tax well ahead of any transaction. And you also need a broker or an investment banker to help you negotiate the sales transaction. Those advisors are very specialized; they're in the market every day and understand value, and they may not be the team you've had before. So you really need to consider that.

Secondly, if you are not good at planning, don't see the need for planning, or have never been through a transaction in your life, please consider a strategic plan for a three to four-year period to not only grow the value of your company but plan the steps of your exit. You don't know what you don't know. There are experts to sit with you at the table and help you every step of the way. This is not the time to throw caution to the win - be measured in your approach to avoid disappointment!

How can people find you, connect with you, and learn more?

Stephen Cummings: Our website is www.rizolve.ca. My cell phone number is 1-416-561-8557. You can easily find me through Google and LinkedIn (https://www.linkedin.com/in/stephenlcummings/).

STEPHEN CUMMINGS

MANAGING PARTNER AND CEO
RIZOLVE PARTNERS INC.

Stephen is the Managing Partner of a leading Strategic Business Advisory Firm to the lower mid-market. A financial expert and strategist who works with private company Business Owners to drive value and to put in place transformational strategies that position businesses for exit on optimal terms.

He has a successful track record in the Canadian Private Equity and Venture Capital Industry, managing large portfolios of private companies developing growth strategies, executing transformations, and achieving numerous liquidity events.

Stephen has also conducted numerous successful consulting assignments involving: acquisitions, disposals, financings, reorganizations, turnarounds, and strategic advisory to numerous Owners and CEOs in both the public and private arenas.

Stephen is a Board Director and sought-after public speaker with international credentials being a qualified CPA, CA in Ontario, Canada, and an FCA in England and Wales.

EMAIL:
scummings@rizolve.ca

PHONE:
1-416-561-8557

WEBSITE:
www.rizolve.ca

RICHARD
DVORAK

CONVERSATION WITH RICHARD DVORAK

Richard, you are a private wealth advisor with Ameriprise Financial Services, LLC. Tell us about your work and the people you help.

Richard Dvorak: I've been in the financial services industry for 22 years. And traditionally, I've done financial planning and wealth management for families with a minimum net worth of about $3 million. But one of the things that I've found is that our traditional model doesn't really work for our business owner clients or appeal to what's most valuable to them. I don't want to say the financial services industry fails business owners, but we have a hard time showing value to business owners. We all have products, and it's more of a product-centric approach. For example, if I offer them a 401k, it's an expense. It costs money to set it up, and they must administer it. If I offer buy/sell insurance or key person insurance, it's another expense. Most business owners care deeply about their business. It's their baby, and they care about the value of the business and the value it adds to their family and personal financial goals. So I got involved with exit planning because we can address what is most important to the business owner: the business's value and accelerating the business's value.

Do business owners put a lot of thought into exit planning?

Richard Dvorak: Everyone will exit their business one way or another, voluntarily or involuntarily. You will either die, become disabled, or successfully sell your business. According to recent studies, only about 17% of business owners actually exit on their terms in a successful transition or sale. So when we talk about exit planning, I want to clarify that it's not about selling your business right now. Most business owners I speak to are not looking to sell right now or think they may never sell, so exit planning is more about helping you define the value of your business. What is it worth today? Is that enough to achieve your lifetime financial goals? How much do you need to net to accomplish those goals, like sending your kids to college or being financially independent? For most people, it's all about financial independence and having enough money to live for the rest of their lives without having to work.

So exit planning always starts with finding the value of your business. What's the street value? What would people be willing to pay? You never really know until you go to market. But we can assess the value right now and get a pretty accurate number. Then we help the business owner determine if it is enough to achieve their goals.

Most people don't know the value of their business. They may have a "country club" value, which means their friend Joe at the country club sold his business for X multiple, so they assume they can get at least a specific number based on their revenue or EBITDA. Often I see owners overestimate the value. They are proud of what they have accomplished and should be. But every industry and every business is different. You can't compare your business to someone else's. Knowing the actual value is extremely important because, for most people, the business is their most significant asset. If you are clueless, it's like not knowing the value of your portfolio. How can you achieve your financial goals if you don't know that? You also have to know how much you need net of taxes to create a lifetime income stream, and most people don't know how to calculate that. Based on these numbers, a business owner can decide to exit now or stay and continue to grow the business to meet their future goals better.

What common pitfalls do business owners face if they exit without a plan?

Richard Dvorak: There are many pitfalls I could discuss. But one of the most important has nothing to do with finances. Business owners need to have a life plan for what they will do personally. They may be used to working 60 or even 90 hours a week, and their life *is* their business. They don't really separate the two. Many people can exit successfully from a financial standpoint but do not have a personal plan. They become discontent, disenchanted, and unhappy. So knowing what the next phase of your life will look like is equally as important as financial planning and preparation.

On the financial side, if you want to get the maximum value for your business, you need to consider it from the buyer's standpoint. What will they find attractive? For example, I worked with a business owner who was the primary salesperson, doing $20 million in revenue. So I asked him, "What happens when you're gone? What happens to sales?" He said, "Well, there probably won't be any sales." A potential buyer will see this as a huge risk, and they will not offer a high multiple. So having a sales department or a sales manager and salespeople makes the business more attractive. There are a lot of risks, but it's more about how you optimize the value and see your business through the lens of a buyer.

Richard, what inspired you to get started in this field?

Richard Dvorak: It's been a journey. I've tried different ways to show value to and attract business owners to our firm. We have a consulting business, and we work with teams and businesses. I was looking for ways to really show value to business owners outside of the products I mentioned earlier, like 401ks, buy/sell agreements, and key person insurance. I just never found those to be valuable when I was talking with business owners.

I've always been an entrepreneur myself. I mowed yards starting at 13 years old and did that all through college and made a lot of money doing it. One of my mentors jokes that every entrepreneur had a paper route or mowed lawns. Then my first real job was at a Fortune 500 financial firm, but it was a fully commissioned job. There was no salary. And I've had other businesses along the way. So I've always been an entrepreneur at heart. I enjoy talking with people that are entrepreneurs, and I'm fascinated by them. Entrepreneurs have the most opportunity for wealth creation and wealth growth. Managing money is a significant revenue stream for our business. If we can help somebody transition out of their business and they have $100 million, maybe they'll look to us to help them manage that transition and the money afterward. There are a lot of opportunities if we, as financial advisors, can provide value to entrepreneurs well before they consider exiting.

Is there anything else you would like to share with business owners considering an exit?

Richard Dvorak: Once you assess the value of the business and figure out if there is a "wealth gap" (the gap between what your business is worth and what it needs to be worth to provide for your lifetime income needs or financial goals), there is a middle component. What do I do with this information? If I want to grow the business or grow the value, how do I do that?

Within the Certified Exit Planning Advisor community, many professionals assess a business's strengths and weaknesses and then help the business owner identify what levers they need to pull to increase value. Do I need to become more systemized? Do I need to have a management team? Do I need to have better processes? Do I need to hire salespeople? That's not what I do, but it's a good way to figure out how to increase the value of your business as you prepare to go to market.

Good exit planning is just good business planning. Even if you don't plan to exit for ten years, if your business is stronger, it will be more valuable. And if it's more valuable, you're probably producing more revenue right now. So nothing bad can happen from working with a Certified Exit Planning Advisor.

How can people find you, connect with you, and learn more?

---⊼---

Richard Dvorak: You can Google me by searching "Richard Dvorak + Private Wealth Advisor." My office line is 281-212-2722. I'm also happy to connect with anybody on LinkedIn.

RICHARD DVORAK, CFP®, CLU®, CEPA®

PRIVATE WEALTH ADVISOR, CERTIFIED
FINANCIAL PLANNER™ PROFESSIONAL
AMERIPRISE FINANCIAL SERVICES, LLC

Richard Dvorak is the Managing Director of a Private Wealth Advisory practice that focuses on financial planning and wealth management. His firm helps clients make financial decisions that simplify their lives and give them confidence about achieving their goals through personal and proactive communication and holistic advice.

In 2022, Richard was ranked #15 on the Forbes Best-In-State Wealth Advisors list for Texas. His firm's clients include families and individuals with $3MM + net worths and business owners.

Richard lives in Houston, TX, with his wife Traci and four children.

PHONE:
281-212-2722

JEFFREY
GEORGE

Conversation with Jeffrey George

Jeffrey, you are the founder of Tao Financial. Tell us about your work and the people you help.

---◆---

Jeffrey George: There are many people out there offering financial planning services to employees collecting a paycheck, and unfortunately, most of them are providing the same service to business owners. I figured out pretty quickly that those services weren't designed to solve owner-specific problems and that the advisors who offer them are often limited in what else they can do to help. Having come from a family of small business owners, it really shook me to my core that these people who are working so hard and sacrificing so much are being left "hanging out to dry" when it comes to the kind of advice they really need to succeed.

In reality, most small and medium-sized businesses struggle in at least one of two areas - financial management and/or business development. This can keep them from growing to the next level and becoming truly valuable. I can't do much about business development since I'm not a marketing expert, but I am a financial expert. It seemed only fair that I use that knowledge to help my clients grow in their businesses and personal lives, and I don't mean by selling them life and disability insurance.

My companies specialize in going the extra mile to help business owner clients make it across the finish line in whatever way they intended when they started or took over their business. That manifests in ways you wouldn't initially guess, or at least I didn't. For example, one client decided they wanted to start a joint venture with other investors, so they needed to develop a set of financial projections. Another needed to figure out how to make the numbers work for hiring more staff so they could have a better quality of life. Those are accounting jobs, not traditional financial advice, but it was what they needed to achieve their plan, so I did the math with them. And in the end, it does eventually lead to the question of, "How and when can I retire?"

One thing that makes my services pretty unique is my background in 401(k) and pension plans. I guess I have a different perspective in that sense and focus the exit planning around the owner's needs above and beyond simply selling their business. I'll help them with that too, but it isn't enough for many folks to meet their goals. Statistics show that 80% of businesses don't sell, so I incorporate a lot of "if/then, either/or" frameworks into our discussions. Their business may or may not sell for what the owner wants, but that doesn't mean it has no cash flow. To the extent possible, I want to see every client retire the way they want. If they can't get it by selling their business, we just have to find another way, and clever usage of 401(k) and pension plans is one more way to accomplish that.

You seem to offer a much wider range of services than most financial advisors. What makes you qualified to provide them?

Jeffrey George: It's a bit ironic, actually. I started out planning to be a CPA, so I've got the complete education necessary for the license. About halfway into my degrees, I realized how much I disliked tax returns and audits and decided to go in a different direction with my life. But before that, I spent a ridiculous amount of time learning how to analyze, model, and present company financial information.

From that point, I worked my way through a couple of years in investment banking before changing direction again and starting a career in "institutional investment consulting." It's basically just a fancy title for people who manage investments for large companies; 401(k)s, pensions, and other types of retirement plans. I did that for most of my career before opening my companies, so I'm very well versed in how those plans work and what can be accomplished with them.

On the business valuation and exit planning side, I've actually completed the coursework used to train professionals who produce certified business valuations, which is offered by the NACVA. I don't have the license because I provide enough services as it is, but it definitely gives me a leg up when it comes to understanding what makes a business valuable. I went through similar training with the Exit Planning Institute.

How much thought do business owners
typically put into exit planning?

--- ———————↑——————— ---

Jeffrey George: For the most part, not very much, if any. But it's very much a mindset thing, and everybody's different. There are people who've been in business for 30 years and haven't put any thought into it, and on the other hand, some owners have only been in business for five years and already have plans in place. To some degree, there is hope that younger generations learn from the experiences of an older generation of business owners, but that might just be wishful thinking on my part.

Unfortunately, the people who need the most help often get the least of it. Most business owners specialize in the goods or services their business provides. Very few of them deal with exit planning in any real sense. Add to that the fact that most of them are neck-deep in running the business day-to-day, and you've got a real problem when it comes to exit planning. They don't know what they don't know, they're too overwhelmed to ask, and when they hire a financial advisor or CPA, I think they expect to get advice about what to do with their business from a planning standpoint. Based on my personal experience, many of them end up disappointed. They get a tax return and an investment portfolio, but the deeper questions about business planning often go unaddressed until the owner brings them up. At that point, they've lost a lot of time, and the people they're working with may or may not be the ones who can answer those questions.

Can you give us a 10,000-foot view
of the exit planning process?

--- ⚓ ---

Jeffrey George: There are many different versions that people in the exit planning field will promote. In my mind, I always start with the business owner and a values-based approach. It's not just about money. It's about a person's life, and what does "quality of life" mean to them? What price are they willing to pay to get what they want? Will it be a fair tradeoff?

For example, let's say you promised yourself never to miss one of your child's ball games, concerts, or dance recitals. When you open the business, will missing ball games be an acceptable sacrifice to grow the business? If it isn't, you may need to modify your expectations or look for other solutions. At the end of the day, you're doing all this because there is something that matters to you as a person, and you can't sacrifice the things that are most important to you and expect to achieve the life you wanted in the first place. It isn't a fair tradeoff and most people I've seen who made those sacrifices aren't happy about it. So if someone says, "I want to spend as much time with my family as possible, live a comfortable life and retirement, and I don't care about being a multimillionaire," then who am I to tell them to take out a bunch of debt to grow the business and put in an extra 20 hours on the weekends if that doesn't match up with what they want? We'll just focus on growing the value of the business in line with what you're willing to commit to. On the other hand, if you're committed to growing a valuable business, I'll be your best cheerleader and supporter in helping to accomplish it in a way that stays true to your values.

So, we start with personal values and then look at a reasonable expectation of what the business can be worth based on the business type, the business's scale, and your willingness to do what it takes to grow it bigger. There's a lot of guesswork that goes into it. Honestly, the devil is in the details and the assumptions you use. Everybody would like to imagine a constantly growing economy, low interest rates and inflation, and easy client acquisition. That's the perfect scenario for a high business value. Unfortunately, that's not consistent with reality - you might enjoy those conditions from time to time, but it's doubtful they'll stick around for the whole ride. I try to be conservative with those assumptions because I would rather underestimate and overachieve than the other way around. Clients seem to like that.

Once we have a reasonable estimate of what the business is worth today, and your willingness to invest in future growth, we then focus on creating a financial plan based on how much money you need to achieve the life you want. If the value of the business covers it, great! We just need to add in some diversification to hedge the risk of something going wrong. If it doesn't, we need to develop a plan for where the rest of the money will come from and how to align it with your goals. That, or we need to discuss priorities. Will goals be adjusted down, or will risks be taken and sacrifices made to grow the business? My job is to help you understand each choice's costs and tradeoffs so you can make an informed decision about whether it's worth paying. Each person gets to make their own choice.

Beyond the planning phase, I provide guidance and objectives for increasing business value over time up to the point of sale. How often and regularly this happens really depends on each client and what stage of life they're in. Sometimes, the recommendations being made aren't something I can help implement. In those cases, I have a handful of trusted partners I can recommend to clients to help them along their journey. Over time, it will usually require various experts to get the job done thoroughly.

Jeffrey, what inspired you to get started in this field?

Jeffrey George: My parents are both in the medical field, and one of them owned a business. Despite their intelligence and accomplishments, money was always a point of frustration. Even though they were putting all the work in, they struggled with making the right financial choices to get them where they wanted to go (like most people). Seeing them work so hard and not have someone in their corner to give them sound advice about making the best use of what they earned was painful. I spent most of my career developing this set of skills with the intention of helping my parents retire. They made a lot of sacrifices for my siblings and me, and I felt they were entitled to a happy ending.

About five years ago, my dad exited his business. I discovered then how easy it is for people in the financial services industry to take a transactional approach to working with business owners. The problem with a transactional approach is that nobody wants to be treated like that when it comes to their life and business. The business broker didn't mention that my dad could have sold his business for more if he did X, Y, and Z. They just sold it. The CPA prepared his tax returns for years but never mentioned anything about business planning or preparing to sell the business. The payroll company sold him a poorly-designed retirement plan that failed to accomplish much more than "checking the box" by offering a benefit to his employees - it barely allowed him to save any money for himself. His financial advisor told him to pull money aside and invest it. Each party sold him the service that paid them the quickest and easiest without asking him (or themselves) whether the service they were providing would get the job done. Nobody wants to be on the receiving end of that, ever. Each of them could have shared some insight into what he should have been thinking about in terms of his long-term success as a business owner and person. It wasn't something they were prepared to help him with, and they didn't want to lose the business, so instead, they said nothing.

In my profession, taking a transactional approach to serving business owners leaves a tremendous vacuum of knowledge on the table. Business owners need that information to get the outcomes they want from life. My family didn't have access to that information, and it would have only taken a small effort from any one of those service providers to point them in the right direction. After that experience, I saw a huge opportunity to add value by being a trusted advisor who takes an owner-centric approach.

Is there anything else you would like to share
with business owners considering an exit?

Jeffrey George: Time matters. You should find a way to accomplish what you want at least five to ten years before exiting because not all of it happens quickly. And with any piece of advice you receive, you need to understand the economic incentives of the person providing the advice. Are there potentially other options or solutions that could be out there that they aren't sharing with you? If there's a sense of urgency, is it yours or theirs?

For most people, their home is their biggest asset. For business owners, that isn't always true. The choice to sell your business, both when and how, is one of the most important financial decisions you will make. Don't take it lightly, and don't delegate the responsibility without keeping one hand on the wheel.

How can people find you, connect
with you, and learn more?

Jeffrey George: Don't laugh, but I'm kind of a dinosaur when it comes to social media. I'm working on getting more active on Facebook - my business handle is TaoFiUSA (you can search for it). Otherwise, you can visit my website at www. taofinancialusa.com. You can also reach me by phone at 407-553-8138 or by email at Jeff@Tao-Fi.com.

Investment advisory services are offered through Tao Financial Inc., a registered investment adviser offering advisory services in the State of Florida and other jurisdictions where registered or exempted.

JEFFREY GEORGE, CFA, CEPA

OWNER & FOUNDER
TAO FINANCIAL INC. & TAO CONSULTING LLC

Jeff George is the owner and founder of Tao Financial Inc. and Tao Consulting LLC. With a decorated background in accounting, finance, and portfolio management, he provides small business owners with holistic financial advice and services covering a broad range of needs. Others have described it as an outsourced CFO service that meets the needs of business owners as both entrepreneurs and as people.

He incorporates both personal and business goals when developing recommendations to small and medium-sized business owners regarding major financial decisions they encounter. Examples include critical decisions regarding preparing for business expansions and exits, including value enhancement strategies, risk management, budgeting and cash management, tax deferral strategies, designing and managing employee savings and retirement programs, creating other executive and employee retention programs, business and personal financial planning, and investment management.

Prior to founding Tao Financial, Jeff accumulated years of experience as an investment banking analyst with JPMorganChase, an institutional investment consultant managing over $2 billion in corporate and retirement plan assets, and as a wealth manager and financial planner at a prominent Registered Investment Advisor (RIA). His formal and professional education includes a Bachelor's and Master's degree in Accounting, the Chartered Financial Analyst® (CFA®) professional designation, and formal training in the areas of business valuation and business exit planning through the NACVA and the Exit Planning Institute.

EMAIL:

Jeff@Tao-Fi.com

PHONE:

407-553-8138

WEBSITE:

www.taofinancialusa.com

LEE JACKSON

Conversation with Lee Jackson

Lee, you are a Certified Exit Planning Advisor with LPL Financial. Tell us about your work and the people you help.

Lee Jackson: I started my career at Merrill Lynch over 20 years ago, helping business owners. It has transformed into assisting them to exit their businesses, whether selling, transferring to their children, or transferring to management internally. I have witnessed a large number of companies attempt to sell independently throughout my career without success. So several years ago, I decided to earn a designation that could help business owners through that process, and I've been very pleased with the success.

Do business owners put much thought into exit planning?

Lee Jackson: They really don't, for the most part. The vast majority are working daily to put out fires and manage all the aspects of the business, so they don't have time to think about what's next or how to get there. A large percentage of business owners have most of their net worth tied up in the business. It is important to get the business transferable and maximize the after-tax proceeds for their family. I start with a financial plan that encompasses the value of the business so the owner will have a clear understanding of what they would need to net to support their family. I then turn my focus on the business. I utilize one of the largest online business valuation software companies to rate the owner's company and compare it to companies across the country in key performance indicators. I help create action plans to strengthen areas that create value while educating the owner on what subtracts value in a company. I assist with tax planning as well. Depending on the type of business entity, there could be some benefits to doing tax and charitable planning in advance to lessen the tax exposure.

*What are the most important things for an owner
to consider when exiting their business?*

--- ⚚ ---

Lee Jackson: One of the biggest things is to get a strong management team in place. Many business owners enjoy running the company and being there daily, but becoming less active is essential as you get closer to exiting. If the management team can run the day-to-day operations and develop and initiate action plans to grow the company, that is ideal. The less involved the owner is, the better. Since this does not happen overnight, it is imperative to identify and develop the management team early, even before contemplating an exit. Once they are identified and developed, offer phantom stock that would be awarded after you exit. This is important because the owner's exit can cause stress for top management. They are accustomed to the owners' expectations and management style but may be uncertain of the buyers. If the management team ever considered leaving to form their own company or be recruited by a competitor, now would be the time. Keeping them happy and in place is important as you plan your exit.

In addition, it's imperative to be diligent in tracking and recording processes. A buyer won't know much about the company when they come in. So they need to have access to processes that are written down. Is there a documented process for growth? Be prepared to show comparable results. I am a member of NACVA (National Association of Certified Valuators and Analysts). In a continuing education webinar in April of 2021, the speaker stated, "As measurement goes, so does behavior." Tracking your monthly revenue and cash flow, especially in challenging times, will give you a sense of where costs can be cut and what hurdles may exist to grow the company. I discussed this in a recent podcast on my website and LinkedIn. I take an individualized approach for each company and will develop a plan for growth based on their personnel and needs.

Statistics show that 80% of businesses that go to market never sell. What are the reasons for this?

---✦---

Lee Jackson: I believe it is a lack of planning and an unrealistic view of what the business is worth. Since the owner is passionate about their business, they may become biased regarding what their business is actually worth. It's my job to show what really goes into valuing a business and what buyers may be looking for. By being a CEPA, if I can get involved early enough, I can get the owner to start thinking objectively about their company. Once the owner sees all the facets of exit planning, they become more open to developing action plans to strengthen areas that may need attention. The ultimate goal is a successful transition so the owner can plan the next chapter of their life.

Lee, what inspired you to get started in this field?

Lee Jackson: I have known for a while that I wanted an advanced designation, and I started researching certifications that I resonated with. I have always enjoyed consulting, so I knew that whatever I chose had to center around helping the business owner. I had decided to concentrate my efforts on the business and the owner when I started my career in 1998. When I became a Certified Exit Planning Advisor and did my research on the field, I knew this designation was perfect for me, especially since I had witnessed many of my clients and contacts attempt to sell on their own unsuccessfully throughout the years. Many designations exist, but Certified Exit Planning Advisor (CEPA) aligns best with my mission.

Is there anything else you would like to share with business owners considering an exit?

Lee Jackson: I would say to take exit planning seriously and to start planning sooner than later. There is much more to exit planning than the typical owner thinks, so it makes good business sense to run your business every day as if you could exit at any time. It's been said that 50% of all exits are unplanned. Apart from an unplanned exit, you never know when an unsolicited offer will come calling, and you will want to be prepared. There are several circumstances throughout my career where I witnessed offers that ultimately did not materialize, and the process hardened the owner's heart. A company in the southwest a number of years ago had a legitimate eight-figure offer for the company, but an ongoing dispute between two owners was too big of a hurdle for the buyer. Today the company is worth about 20% of the offering price ten years before. Each year a company will sell for an above-average multiple of EBITDA (Earnings Before Interest, Taxes, Depreciation, and Amortization), and a company will sell for a below-average multiple of EBITDA in the same exact category. The difference could literally be millions of dollars. To me, it is crucial to start taking exit planning seriously and doing the necessary planning well in advance so you will be prepared. It is important for you and your family.

How can people find you, connect
with you, and learn more?

--- ⟳ ---

Lee Jackson: You can call me at 334-676-2288 or visit my website at www.leejacksonlpl.com. I charge a very reasonable monthly retainer. I have instructional videos covering every facet of exit planning on my website at leejacksonlpl.com. My videos are also on LinkedIn, so I encourage you to connect with me there. My email address is Lee.jackson@lpl.com.

Securities and advisory services offered through LPL Financial, A Registered Investment Advisor. Member FINRA/SIPC

LEE JACKSON

CERTIFIED EXIT PLANNING ADVISOR
(CEPA), PRIVATE WEALTH ADVISOR
LPL FINANCIAL

Lee is a Certified Exit Planning Advisor (CEPA) and Private Wealth Advisor with LPL Financial and has assisted business owners and their families since 1998. Lee obtained a CEPA designation to help owners navigate through each stage of the exit process. Lee is trained to rate the attractiveness of the business and helps create action plans to increase the business value while making sure the owner is personally prepared to exit. Lee utilizes business valuation software to rate the company's key performance measures and compare it to similar companies nationwide. To help the owner understand what they will need to support their retirement lifestyle, Lee uses financial planning software that encompasses the value of the business and illustrates ways to limit tax exposure by utilizing charitable trusts or donor-advised funds.

Lee has numerous informative videos on LinkedIn covering important areas of exit planning. Feel free to reach out and connect on LinkedIn. He has a degree from Auburn University at Montgomery and resides in Montgomery, Alabama.

Lee is married and has a son who is attending Huntingdon College. Lee enjoys spending time with his family, church, pets, sports, and cooking meals for the homeless.

EMAIL:
Lee.jackson@lpl.com

PHONE:
334-676-2288

WEBSITE:
www.leejacksonlpl.com

R.J. KELLY

CONVERSATION WITH R.J. KELLY

R.J., you are the founder and Chief Visionary
Officer of Wealth Legacy Group®, Inc. Tell us
about your work and the people you help.

--- ⚓ ---

R.J. Kelly: To understand what I do and why I do it, it's important to know where I came from. My father died when I was eighteen. He had built a multimillion-dollar company but, unfortunately, had not invested in his own management team to the degree he had invested in plant & equipment. Things were fine when the business was at a certain level of success. But things weren't so fine when it had grown to a higher level of success and complexity. You see, when the visionary dies, unless they have enabled and grown a team behind them, the business dies as well. Ten years after my father's death, the company was bankrupt. Fortunately, my parents had done some farsighted asset protection planning which enabled us to keep the family ranch and a few other assets, but we lost everything else.

That became the impetus for me to build a firm that can sit down with financially successful individuals, especially business families that have not sold or transitioned their business yet. We help them think through the various aspects of their planning. Not just estate planning, wills & trusts, insurance, investments, retirement, and income needs – as important as they are - but also their legacy. What do they want to leave for their kids? And what do they want to leave for their community - if anything? To do that takes a very diverse firm like Wealth Legacy Group® to address all these issues at more than just a superficial level. In my 35-plus years of practice, I have never met anyone like us with the breadth of disciplinary scope, but that can also go very deep. Other professional planning firms may be skilled in their particular discipline, but ask them two or three questions outside of that skill set, and they won't have a good answer.

Armando Christian Pérez, better known as the artist "Pitbull," says, "Always stay an intern." Always keep growing. Always be learning. Always stay inquisitive. I'm a Certified Exit Planning Advisor with a whole bunch of other letters after my name because I want to keep growing as a person. I also want to bring my best to every client engagement, especially privately held business owners, because their needs are invariably complex and multifaceted.

Do business owners put a lot of thought into exit planning?

R.J. Kelly: Thought? Perhaps. Actually creating an exit plan? Rarely!

There's a wonderful group called Vistage and other excellent peer networking groups like Sage, EO, YPO, Renaissance Executive Forums, etc. These groups exist to help coach each other, but also, they're facilitated by an extraordinary business mentor.

I have spoken for many of these groups, and they frequently remind members (as do I) to follow Stephen Covey's advice: "Begin with the end in mind." That is, decide on your exit plan when you first open your doors. Most business owners, however, just give it lip service. They think, "Yeah, right. I am just trying to have enough money left to make payroll this week! Exit plan? Shmexit plan!"

Business owners have more coming at them today in terms of complexity and things demanding their attention than any time I can recall in nearly 40 years. It's no wonder they haven't made time to create an exit plan, and most assume that it will be a long way off.

Research shows that most business owners spend more time planning a vacation than their business exit! To be fair, some of this comes from not knowing whom to trust, where to go, or what questions to ask. They also don't usually wake up in the morning saying to themselves, "Gosh, I could die or become permanently disabled today. We better figure out how to handle those contingencies."

What is the role of an exit planning advisor?

R.J. Kelly: In our case, what I bring as an exit planning advisor is outside perspective and knowledge of how the various planning disciplines intersect. I also usually have a greater knowledge of the participants and their families to bring to the creative discussion with the attorney and any other advisors involved. For example ...

I was contacted several years ago by a gentleman who was a partner in a national homebuilding company. It's a brilliant company. They make beautiful homes in a vibrant and growing part of the country for shockingly low prices compared to California prices. As successful and bright as these two partners are, however, they had never gotten around to putting together a buy/sell agreement. Frankly, this is not uncommon. If one of the partners was not dying, it might not have risen to the level of importance it did. Often it is because they don't really know where to begin. They engaged us to sit down, clarify their goals and help put a buy-sell agreement together, which, by the way, actually became TWO separate agreements.

We start with asking a LOT of questions, beginning with the obvious of how much money they each wanted upon death, disability, or retirement - how soon - with whom to represent the surviving families in the event of the death or disability of one or both of the partners, and so forth. I brought in an outstanding business attorney in San Diego named Troy. Between us, we identified and addressed the various issues and complexities for the two partners and hammered out those agreements.

A quick point of clarification. While I have an attorney on staff, and we review documents regularly, we don't draft them. Again, my point in bringing that up is that I bring an outside perspective without a potential conflict in objectivity that could come if we were also drafting the documents through our firm.

I have studied what my father went through and where he went wrong and have worked with hundreds of other business owners over my career. I know the 17 questions (at a minimum) that need to be answered. Not to take anything away from attorneys, but unless drafting buy-sell agreements is something they routinely do, I find things are inevitably left out of the agreement that should be included.

But, in addition to the pure technical decisions of whether to have a cross-purchase - entity - trusteed cross-purchase - "Hewlett Packard" buy-sell or something else ... we add one other ingredient to the mix. We have taken the time to understand the business owner's goals and family situation as well or better than any other advisor. Without that understanding, attorneys have made suggestions that could strait-jacket the survivors and are not what the partner wanted for their spouse and family or business partner(s).

For example, many buy/sell agreements don't address or address thoroughly enough the issue of: "What happens if one of the partners becomes totally or permanently disabled?" Not only do we need to value the business, but as of what date? How do we measure certain items or value inventory? When does a buyout occur in the event of a disability? Who determines if it IS a disability? And so on. I call it the "missing pages" in most buy/sell agreements. Again, it takes a team, and you can't simply rely on your attorney and your CPA. You really need someone who's trained like myself and others who are Certified Exit Planning Advisors.

As a quick aside but important comment, there are two organizations in the exit planning space that train advisors. One is BEI - Business Enterprise Institute - and the other is EPI - the Exit Planning Institute. My designation is through EPI, but they're both outstanding programs for training advisors who are serious about wanting to help business owners plan their exit. So, if you are a business owner looking to exit, make sure at least one member of your planning team has received the BEI or EPI exit planner certification.

R.J., what inspired you to get started in this field?

R.J. Kelly: Trust me, it was not even remotely on my radar screen! As already mentioned, my father died when I was eighteen. I was in my first month of university. Out of loyalty to my family, I would have quit school to help the family except for a conversation my dear mom had with me a year before my father's unexpected death. She simply told me, "Honey, we would love to have you in the family business if you want to be here. Frankly, I'm not even sure the family business is the right place for you. I think you are meant to explore other interests and bigger challenges. Regardless, your father and I just want you to know that the decision is yours, and we will support your decision, whatever that is."

I don't remember saying much or even processing the conversation much at that point. A year later, though, when my father died, I went back home to be with my family with my mother's words in my head. As usual, she was right. I was not enamored with the family business - successful as it was – and could not picture myself working there for a lifetime. Because of my mom's encouragement to consider other avenues, I decided to stay in school, get my degree, and pursue other career opportunities. I considered becoming a marriage and family therapist to make a difference in the lives of families and individuals at a personal level. First, though, I wanted to taste the business world. After all, I had grown up as the son of an entrepreneur, so the thrill of being self-employed was in my DNA.

I have four world filters that guide my decisions. First and foremost is that I'm a follower of Jesus. So, I asked myself, "Lord, what do you want me to do? Where can I apply the skills and talents you have given me in a way that honors you, blesses others, and is fun and challenging for me? I discovered to my surprise that a career in financial services could satisfy my desire to be an entrepreneur and make a positive difference in the lives of others. Here I am today, over 35 years later, more in love with what I do professionally than ever!

In an ironic twist, I turned down a job opportunity with Procter and Gamble because they wanted me to move to Southern California. I thought, "There's no way I'm moving to Southern California from Washington State." Lo and behold, in 1985, I started my "Abraham adventure" (as in Abraham in the Old Testament when God called him away from where he lived to a new place for unnamed reasons.) We moved to San Diego, where I knew exactly one person, and started over again! We now have clients in over 19 states, but for us, there is no place like San Diego.

While I am here, may I make one other quick point? There's a saying, "God won't steer a parked car." You need to be moving to be "steerable." As I prepared to graduate university, the professional direction seemed clear to me. Instead, my loving Heavenly Father had something bigger for me - taking me somewhere quite different than I planned, but into something I wanted in my heart-of-hearts.

Through a series of events, I was given the opportunity to enter the life insurance business. Frankly, I couldn't have been LESS interested in something like that, or so I thought at the time. It was like asking me if I would like to be a concert pianist. Well, music is in my background, but I didn't want to spend my life doing it. And there is also that troublesome aspect of needing the talent to compete at the level where I could make a difference. But I began to see that the life insurance profession would allow me to be in business for myself, which I was attracted to as the son of an entrepreneur. At the same time, I could also be in a business where I could make a meaningful difference in the lives of others, both individual families and their businesses.

My practice has evolved and morphed a great deal over time. Over 60% of our revenue now comes from advising clients on how best to grow and protect their money and income. Insurance makes up a far smaller percentage of our income, but it is still a meaningful aspect of what we do. This is especially true now that we've discovered certain banks are willing to pay the premiums for some of our more affluent clients.

In addition, we have our standalone financial consulting service to address the frequent disconnect between a client's estate and asset protection planning (if they have even done something to address this), insurance, investments, income planning, and their legacy and philanthropic wishes. Most just have "vague intentions" of what they want to do overall but have not made the time to create an integrated and comprehensive plan - just like my parents failed to do. We get hired to do that, and what a personal thrill that is for me to help, regardless of whether we also help clients manage their investments or help with the purchase of needed insurance products – both aspects that can come as a by-product of consulting work.

Our tax mitigation practice for those selling appreciated assets like real estate and businesses has exploded in growth. In those cases, the seller(s) are *extremely* interested to learn ways to reduce, defer and, in some cases, even *eliminate* the taxes on the sale of the appreciated asset(s). With COVID restrictions lifting and finding ourselves all two years older, we are inundated with folks wanting to get to the sidelines and enjoy life. When they find out they will pay 37%, 39%, 50%+, or even "just" 24% in taxes, they want to understand the alternatives Congress has put into the tax code decades before – some over 50 years prior!

Most other advisors either don't know some of these IRS code sections and the tax relief available or DO know but don't know how to introduce and integrate the strategies. We do, and this is presently bringing in two to three new cases per week.

We have never been so busy as now in this area of practice - helping others understand that the U.S. government allows us to choose how to support the "social well-being" of our country. It is possible to make capital gains taxes and estate/inheritance taxes "optional"... and NOT go to jail.

Paying more in taxes than is necessary is not somehow patriotic, or even sensible for that matter. By supporting the country in a way that aligns with the seller's values, opting out of paying capital gains taxes and estate or inheritance taxes is not only permitted by Congress through the tax code but also *encouraged!*

I know ... pretty radical thinking from what most people are told by their advisors that they "just have to bite the bullet and pay the taxes." That is simply NOT true, but the planning does have to be done in advance of the liquidity event for the biggest tax savings to be realized.

One more "P.S." It is possible to reduce taxes even AFTER a taxable liquidity event, as long as the "tax-offset" planning happens in the same year as the liquidity event. We saved a sweet older couple over $1.2 million in taxes by implementing two strategies post-sale in the same tax year as their sale. They still had to pay $927,000 when it could have been zero had they found us before selling the assets. Nonetheless, they were thrilled to give the IRS and Franchise Tax Board $1.2 million less now and send that money to support philanthropic causes they believe in once they are both gone.

Wealth Legacy Group®, Inc. has grown from just me years ago to now include seven full-time or part-time members of the "tribe," without which I simply could not do what I do. I am so thankful to them, especially to my remarkable wife, Vymean, our COO, who directs the backstage while I do what I do frontstage. With this wonderful talent supporting me, we can sit down with that successful business owner or professional or executive and help take what are often vague intentions about their business succession, family, money, philanthropy, and legacy - and help them become very specific, measurable, and meaningful decisions.

Earlier I mentioned two partners in a dynamic and vertically integrated homebuilding company. We helped them put two buy-sell agreements into place. Tragically, one of the two partners passed away just two weeks after signing the second agreement and finalizing his estate planning documents. Extremely successful, bright, caring, with a lovely family, he had just never gotten around to prioritizing his estate planning, and it was almost too late. Because of his sheer mental tenacity, deep love for his family, and the committed application of skills by the estate attorney and us, we got the job done just in time to ensure his family would be taken care of. I also think the good Lord answered our prayers and gave him a little more time to be with his family and for us to make sure all the planning was in place.

How can people find you, connect
with you, and learn more?

- - - ————✦———— - - -

R.J. Kelly: Go to our website and start the "sniff and smell" test. You can find the brightest people in the world, but if you don't resonate with them, you shouldn't work with them. Our website is www.wealthlegacygroup.com.

Or, send a personal email to me at rj@wealthlegacygroup. com. Please put "Urgent" in the subject line, as I receive hundreds of emails daily. We offer a 20-minute complimentary conversation to discuss anything you want, including suggestions for investing in these turbulent times, buy/sell agreements, estate planning, asset protection, or how to reduce, defer or eliminate capital gains tax or estate tax – whatever is keeping you awake at night, or you are wondering about.

We have also created several complimentary informational articles and videos to send business owners considering an exit. There is no obligation, and nobody will follow up with them unless they ask for follow-up. They can reach me directly at rj@wealthlegacygroup.com, ask for materials on "preparing for an exit," and we will be happy to send them.

In summary, let's identify any "vague intentions" about your business, your wealth, your family, your legacy, and potentially your philanthropy that have not yet been acted upon, and let us help you implement those intentions in very specific, measurable and meaningful ways – along with periodically reviewing them to keep them up-to-date as family and business situations and tax laws change!

Thank you for the privilege of being included on your program and in this collection with other outstanding contributors. It is a great honor to be a part of, and I hope readers find this book helpful in realizing a successful exit!

R.J. KELLY, ChFC, CLU, MSFS, IAR, CAP, RICP, AEP, WMCP, CEPA

FOUNDER AND CHIEF VISIONARY OFFICER
WEALTH LEGACY GROUP, INC.

R.J. Kelly is the founder and Chief Visionary Officer of Wealth Legacy Group®, Inc. in San Diego, California, a company specializing in the diverse financial and planning needs of successful entrepreneurs, professionals, executives, and their families.

His father built a multi-million business but tragically died when R.J. was only eighteen. Within ten years of his father's death, the business was shuttered and in bankruptcy. Without an integrated financial and succession plan, the business and family wealth was lost, along with the jobs of dozens of employees. This created a passion for R.J. to build a multi-disciplinary approach to address the complex and often competing needs/issues of successful business families and wealthy/affluent individuals and their families.

As a result, R.J. created the proprietary *Critical Actions Roadmap*™ by which he and the WLG "tribe" develop comprehensive plans that:

- Facilitate successful business succession and exit outcomes
- Maximize investment and asset growth
- Mitigate risk using various insurance and asset protection strategies
- Create clarity in family legacy & issues of philanthropy

R.J. has been a financial advisor for over 35 years and is a:

- Chartered Financial Consultant®
- Chartered Life Underwriter®
- Retirement Income Certified Professional®

- Chartered Advisor in Philanthropy®

- Wealth Management Certified Professional®, trained in the intersection of retirement planning and wealth management skills to address the complex needs of financially successful clients

- IAR of Wealth Legacy Group®, Inc., an independent Registered Investment Advisor

Additionally, R.J. has a(n):

- Master's in financial services with an emphasis on tax mitigation

- Accredited Estate Planner (AEP®) designation recognizing a graduate-level specialization in estate planning

- Certified Exit Planning Advisor designation through an executive MBA-style program that trains and certifies qualified professional advisors in the field of exit planning for business owners

R.J. is also a frequent speaker and writer, and is the author of the upcoming book, *Creating Your Ideal Retirement – Starting Today!*

EMAIL:
rj@wealthlegacygroup.com

PHONE:
(858) 569-0633

WEBSITE:
www.wealthlegacygroup.com

MARK
KRAVIETZ

Conversation with Mark Kravietz

Mark, you are the founder of ALINE Wealth. Tell us about your work and the people you help.

Mark Kravietz: I help business owners prepare for an exit and post-exit and help them replace the income they will miss from the business they sell. I've helped over 100 business owners, families, and others get ready to move into their next phases of life, leaving their businesses for something else they really love and enjoy doing. I typically work with middle-market business owners selling their company for the first time or passing the business down to their children. I help guide them down the tricky path to help them successfully sell their business.

How much thought do business owners
put into exit planning?

Mark Kravietz: Not enough. I sit with many business owners and ask them about their exit strategies. Most of them don't have one. They just think, "Hey, I'm making good money, so I'll just keep this up." But if you think about it, an exit strategy is really a business strategy. I've talked to owners who thought they wanted to exit their business, but as we have analyzed their business, it turns out they want to grow their business to a much higher level and exit later. This is a key fork in the road for many business owners. They are not sure if they want to sell or expand. Going through the exit planning process is an excellent way for the owner to come to a conclusion.

Are there preconceived notions about selling a business?

Mark Kravietz: There are a few preconceived notions about selling a business. First, many owners think of their businesses like their babies. They feel they own a great business, and people will line up to buy the company when they are ready to sell. In many cases, they have a good business, but it takes a village and a period of time to sell a business. I would recommend starting the process three years in advance. This will give ample time to put the business in the best position to sell, or if an opportunity comes along sooner, you will be in a more ready position to sell.

A second preconceived notion is that the owner can sell the company themselves. In most cases, this is the first time you're selling your business. You might be selling to someone that has done this many times before. They will look to take advantage of the situation. It would be in your best interest to get the best professional help you can find. After all, this will be the biggest and most important transaction of your life. So you want to make sure you have the best advice available.

The last and maybe the most important preconceived notion is that the business owner is identified with their company. If they sell, they will lose their identity. This has stopped many owners in the past from maximizing the value of their company. Owners have to look at their priorities and determine what they want. If they can sell their company and put money away for their own lifestyle and future generations, this opportunity might not come along again. We see companies hang on too long and lose the ability to create liquid wealth for themselves and their families.

What value do exit planners provide to business owners?

———✦———

Mark Kravietz: I'm President of the Greater New York chapter of the Exit Planning Institute. The Exit Planning Institute helps practitioners understand and help business owners get ready to go through an exit. So we believe in education, and one part of that education is the three legs of the stool a business owner needs. What are those legs? Number one: Ensure you're personally and financially prepared. Number two: Maximize the value of your business. Number three: Understand what you will do after you sell your business.

Many business owners don't think about that last part. As I mentioned, the owners are typically known for their work and are deeply connected to the business. Understanding what they are going to do next is a dynamic process. Quite frankly, many business owners are unhappy after selling. According to a Pricewaterhouse study, 12 months after selling, three out of four business owners surveyed "profoundly regretted" the decision to sell. They may have received the price they wanted, but they have no idea what to do with themselves. So, a big part of our process is helping them ensure they have a plan after the sale.

How has the recent pandemic affected your market?

Mark Kravietz: I have a very popular podcast called "Find Your Exit." I interview business owners about the trials and tribulations of exiting their businesses. During the pandemic, I pivoted and interviewed owners on how they were faring during this once-in-a-lifetime event. The key element to success was pivoting. They had to use ingenuity and flexibility to get through that difficult time. For example, I interviewed Andrew Alfano, CEO of Retro Fitness. Retro Fitness has over 150 gym locations. At the time, nobody was going to the gym. He pivoted and created classes that the members could do at home. In addition, he added nutritional tips and educated the members on many areas of healthcare. This bridged the gap until people started to come back to the gym. It also led to Project LIFT, a new company initiative to open 500 health clubs in 50 Black and Brown communities across the country over the next five years.

Mark, what inspired you to get started in this field?

Mark Kravietz: It's really a personal story. My dad came here from another country virtually penniless. He started working in the garment industry in Manhattan as a runner. Over time he moved up in his company and started his business with a partner. He ran a typical small business with about 15 employees. Unfortunately, most of the garment industry left the country and went to China. My dad was forced to liquidate the company. It was a very difficult time for my dad and our family, where I saw all of the pain my dad went through. And after that, I wanted to dedicate my time and effort to helping business owners avoid the same exit as my dad. I am very passionate about helping business owners get the right exit they deserve.

Is there anything else you would like to share with business owners considering an exit?

Mark Kravietz: People don't plan to fail; they just fail to plan. This is a complex process, and you need to have a plan. Here are some process suggestions.

First, think about what you will do with yourself post-sale. Make sure you plan for all that newfound time on your hands. There are no perfect times to sell, but regardless of what's happening in the outside world, sell when your business is on an upswing. Once you decide to sell, bring on the best-experienced professionals to help you with this process. This could include a business attorney, Certified Exit Planner, wealth manager experienced with business owners, business accountant, investment banker, M&A advisor, business broker, business valuation expert, and many more, depending on your business.

It takes a village to sell a company.

Figure out what your number is. Most owners will overstate the value of their company. It's important to do a personal cash flow analysis to look at what realistic number you need to continue living the same lifestyle and stay in that lifestyle for the rest of your life. Make sure you get multiple offers, as this can increase your company's value. Be careful of earnouts. When you get an offer, determine what your role will be post-sale. There are so many more factors. Start by creating a plan and sticking to it.

How can people find you, connect with you, and learn more?

Mark Kravietz: My website is www.alinewealth.com. You can also email me directly at mkravietz@alinewealth.com.

ALINE Wealth is a group of investment professionals registered with Hightower Securities, LLC, member FINRA and SIPC, and with Hightower Advisors, LLC, a registered investment advisor with the SEC. Securities are offered through Hightower Securities, LLC; advisory services are offered through Hightower Advisors, LLC.

MARK KRAVIETZ,
CIMA®, CFP®, CEPA

MANAGING PARTNER/FOUNDER
ALINE WEALTH, HIGHTOWER ADVISORS

Mark Kravietz is the Managing Partner and Founder of ALINE Wealth. Mark offers financial solutions with a decidedly human touch. He brings a consummate investment acumen to the full range of clients' challenges, supplemented by considerable insight into exit strategy. His financial, investment, and exit planning knowledge has helped clients through difficult economic and market cycles. "I help clients every step of the way in their success," he says, "from building it to sharing it with their loved ones when that time comes."

Mark holds the Certified Financial Planner (CFP®) designation and the Certified Investment Management Analyst (CIMA®) designation from the Wharton School of Business. He specializes in exit planning and achieved the prestigious accreditation of Certified Exit Planning Advisor (CEPA) from the University of Chicago's Booth Business School. He is a founding member and President of the New York Chapter of the Exit Planning Institute (EPI). Mark has been recognized for efforts in exit planning with EPI's 2016 Leader of the Year award at the Exit Planning Institute's International Conference and was honored in 2014 with the Excellence in Planning and Volunteer of the Year Award.

Mark was named among the top wealth advisors in New York state from 2019-2022 by Forbes Magazine. He was selected by the Long Island Business News (LIBN) as a 2021 Business and Finance Award winner. He has been the subject of articles in various publications and has made radio appearances. Mark also has a podcast about how to successfully exit your business called "Find Your Exit" and a video series called "Coffee With Krav."

EMAIL:
mkravietz@alinewealth.com

PHONE:
(631) 760-7636

WEBSITE:
www.alinewealth.com

LINKEDIN:
https://www.linkedin.com/in/markkravietz/

MICHAEL LIVIAN

CONVERSATION WITH MICHAEL LIVIAN

Michael, you are the founder of Livian & Co. Tell us about your work and the people you help.

---✦---

Michael Livian: We are wealth managers and exit planners. Our specialty is working with business owners and entrepreneurs. We have focused on this space for about 12 years. Our clients are spread throughout the entire country. We also have international clients in Europe and South America, generally wealthy entrepreneurs who are self-made and built their businesses from the ground up. Typically, we deal with multi-generational wealth shared by parents, children, and grandchildren. So we help them plan the succession, including business planning, wealth management, tax optimization, and defining and designing a legacy.

How much thought do business owners
put into exit planning?

Michael Livian: Most successful business owners think they have an exit plan because they have given consideration to the future of their business. However, most don't fully appreciate what an exit plan entails. They know they want to monetize the value of their business or pass it on to their heirs. But they don't know all the pitfalls, tax issues, fees, and stumbling blocks involved. It's very daunting for someone who has been working hard to build a business to get to the level of technical expertise needed to exit successfully. That's where we come into play. We have studied and mastered the best practices and processes required for a successful transition.

Are there common misconceptions about selling a business?

Michael Livian: Owners' greatest misconception is how much their business is worth. A private business is similar to someone's home: because of its "emotional" value, almost everyone overestimates its market value. Moreover, with a business, most owners don't realize that part of that value may be paid in taxes and fees when monetized. So the most important things at the beginning of the process are to examine the business's strengths and weaknesses, run the preliminary valuation, and explain the transaction's tax consequences and the intermediaries' cost. This will give the business owner more of a realistic number. Then we go over strategies to increase and grow the value of the business to its fullest potential.

Ultimately, parting ways with a business you have built is a very emotional decision. It entails a lot. It is a life-changing event, and you must carefully consider what you will do after your business sells. Sometimes owners shy away from selling because they realize they may be sitting on a big bank account, but they won't know what to do with themselves. Entrepreneurs typically have dynamic personalities. They can't sit down and stay idle; they need action. So we also work with business owners to develop a life plan to address a transition's emotional aspects.

When is the best time to start preparing for an exit?

Michael Livian: Over years of practice and participating in study groups with The Exit Planning Institute, we have learned that the typical lead time for an exit is two years. An exit plan is like a business plan. You write the business plan when you start the business and then regularly update it each year. It's an ongoing plan with an ongoing budget. An exit plan should start the same way and also be ongoing. To be successful at anything in life, you need to think ahead and you need to plan. So it's not something you would do a month before; it's not simply looking for a buyer. That's not an exit plan.

Michael, what inspired you to get started in this field?

Michael Livian: I got started because I realized the vast majority of our wealth management clients were business owners with similar issues. They had concerns and worries and seemed to need help. I saw very successful people with significant wealth being anxious about the future: what to do with their money, their children, and their business, especially at a time when technology is shortening product cycles and the life cycles of businesses. Every business is continuously under the threat of innovation and disruptive changes. Helping business owners with succession planning was practically an outgrowth of our existing wealth management business. Then I realized there was a whole universe of possibilities. Our services are valuable because every entrepreneur needs an exit plan, and very few have one.

*Is there anything else you would like to share
with business owners considering an exit?*

Michael Livian: I believe most business owners need an exit plan to protect and harvest the value of their business. But they may be a little hesitant to take the necessary steps because they are always busy. As a business owner, getting sucked into your day-to-day activities is very easy, and it's difficult to think strategically. However, the most critical thing for every business owner is to think forward.

And that may not be an exit. An exit plan is also a contingency plan. Most business owners are unlikely to think about random occurrences that could affect their business. So part of an exit plan is ensuring the value of the business is protected in case of death, disability, dispute, distress, or divorce (the famous five "Ds"). Several situations may derail a plan or even push a business into liquidation. These can be prevented, or at least mitigated, by having an exit plan. An exit plan includes a proactive growth-oriented component aiming to increase the value of the business and to prepare you for a succession, but there is also a component about risk management. You need to have risk management in place.

How can people find you, connect
with you, and learn more?

Michael Livian: Our website is www.livianco.com. You can also email us at info@livianco.com. Our office number is 212-319-8900.

MICHAEL LIVIAN, CFA, CEPA

FOUNDER
LIVIAN & CO.

Michael Livian is the founder and CEO of Livian & Co. He has over 26 years of experience in the financial services industry, working with entrepreneurs, high net-worth families, and a wide range of institutions. Previously, he was the Executive Managing Director at Safdie Investment Services Corp. (subsidiary of the Swiss private bank, Banque Safdie) and a Managing Director at Speed Ventures, a primary pan-European private equity/VC firm. He also worked as an Associate Director for Bear Stearns & Co. in New York and Italy, with a special focus on fixed income and credit derivatives. He holds a summa cum laude MSc degree in Economics from the University of Milan. He published several academic articles and books on quantitative finance, fixed income, and equity valuation. He is a CFA charter holder, a CFA Society of New York (CFASNY) member, and a Certified Exit Planning Advisor (CEPA). He lives in New York with his wife and three children.

EMAIL:
mlivian@livianco.com

PHONE:
(212) 319-8900

WEBSITE:
www.livianco.com

PAUL A. KYRIMIS

CONVERSATION WITH PAUL A. KYRIMIS

Paul, you are the founder of Legacy Global Strategies. Tell us about your work and the people you help.

--- ⚜ ---

Paul A. Kyrimis: We work with business owners who are probably not even considering exiting, and exit planning is only part of what we do with small business owners. Your business must transition before you exit. The transition focuses on maximizing the value of your business and may take 2 to 5 years to complete, and the result is a business that runs so efficiently the current owner may not want to sell! This transition process leads to improved EBITDA and increased multiples, creating a more attractive business with improved readiness when the exit occurs. Our ideal client is in the lower middle market, with annual revenue between $5 million and $100 million. Our sweet spot is that $10 million to $50 million range, but that doesn't mean we won't work with lower revenue business owners. In fact, we are gearing up a program right now to help owners who want to grow from the lower revenue market. We try to make our services affordable because those owners are the ones who need our help the most to grow and maximize the business value long before the eventual sale.

How much thought do business owners put into exit planning?

Paul A. Kyrimis: Entrepreneurs and business owners are very intelligent people. They are good at what they do. They are the perfect COO for the business as they know all the ins and outs of the widget, process, or system they are providing to their clients. Because they are so devoted to running the business, they don't have time to make a plan for getting out or even reducing the long hours they are working. We use the phrase "transition" to describe the enhancements needed before the business is attractive to a potential buyer. For example, the business needs to stand and grow independently without the owner. The owners who wear all the hats, don't delegate responsibility, or have not focused on building the right team/culture will ultimately have difficulty selling the business. We ask the owner, "What would your business look like if you had NO contact with the business for 60 days, 90 days, 120 days, or more? What would you come back to?" The answer is overwhelming, along the lines of, "Much less than I have now, if anything at all." We follow up with, "Would you like to be able to take time off, for any length of time, for any reason you want, and know that you will return to a strong business and potentially more than when you left?" The answer is something to the effect of, "Paul, I'm listening."

Can you give us a 10,000-foot view
of the exit planning process?

Paul A. Kyrimis: We begin with an assessment that takes about 90 days to complete. During this assessment, we look at all the business strategies (i.e., sales, marketing, finance, accounting, human resources, intellectual property, IT, legal, etc.). Each of these strategies needs to run as close to 100% efficiency as possible. We create a list of enhancements from the assessment and order them according to priority level.

Then we look at the internal talent pool within the business. For example, let's say it's a human resources issue, perhaps the HR assessment scored 58%. So we focus on that gap between 58 and 100. We look internally to their HR department. If they don't have anybody internally that can proceed through the next 90 days to correct the HR situation; we ask the owner if they know anyone who can step into that role. If not, we have professionals who can fill this gap. It's important to attempt to find someone the owner knows, likes, and trusts so they are more comfortable with the process. If we go outside the business for an interim/consultant, we will provide a few recommendations for the type of advisor required for the owner to interview.

We also communicate to the current internal staff that the company's transition is potentially beneficial to them, as this may be their opportunity to display their talents to become a "highly trusted" and integral part of the company's future!

After 90 days (typically), we have completed the HR concern and moved to the next priory enhancement. The process is repeated every 90 days until we have exhausted the enhancement discovered during the assessment process and the company is maintaining its level of maximized value.

When is the best time to start exit planning?

--- ——————🔾—————— ---

Paul A. Kyrimis: Ideally, starting a business with the end in mind is always valuable. When starting a business, there are so many things the new owner is consumed with; the "end" is not even on the list. It's very important to begin the value maximization process from the get-go, which is always what I think when I work with "under $5 million" businesses. We relate this question to the more common question, "When do you start planning for your retirement?" The answer is "as soon as possible and well ahead of your retirement date!" This is truly important to the business owner, as the sales proceeds from the business can, by some estimates, make up more than 90% of the retirement dollars the owner will need during retirement! It's never too late to correct and improve. As I mentioned, the owners who try to do everything are the biggest issue. If things can't run on their own without the owner helicoptering around on a daily basis, potential buyers will not be interested in paying for the business and working 70 to 100 hours a week.

Paul, what inspired you to get started in this field?

Paul A. Kyrimis: I worked with small business owners for almost a decade from a financial aspect. In 2016, two different business owners came to me after the fact and said, "Paul, I sold my business. I would like you to meet the new owners." Because I wasn't aware of nor involved with the current owner's desire to sell, the new business owners had obtained advisors during the exit process, who they trusted, and I was excused from my advisor role. As you might imagine, these two harsh realities sparked my interest!

Then in 2017, I attended an event called The Gathering at Southern California Institute (SCI), headed by Joe Strazzeri and his highly talented team (Strazzeri Mancini LLP in CA). SCI does a fantastic job of pulling together advisors and centers of influence who business owners should be involved with, including various attorneys, CPAs, wealth managers, etc. It was there I met Chris and Scott Snider for the first time, who are the owners of the Exit Planning Institute. That's where I was exposed to the details of everything a business owner must know to achieve maximum value in their business before a successful exit may be achieved. I decided that instead of being pushed out of the way once a sale was made, I wanted to be ahead of that wave, create a deeper relationship as a trusted advisor, and maintain my business with that particular client. So it made sense to obtain my CEPA (Certified Exit Planning Advisor) certification in 2017. It's been a great experience.

*Is there anything else you would like to share
with business owners considering an exit?*

---⬥---

Paul A. Kyrimis: From my experience talking with business owners, the different ways to exit are not clear to them. There are nine ways to consider, whether an IPO or actually shuttering the business, with seven options in between. In addition, downside events might force you out of your business, such as the 5 Ds (death, divorce, disability, disillusionment, and distress). Distress can be economic distress, most recently, the last few years during and after the Covid pandemic. All of these options of exiting will affect the value of your business. Another option is the "unsolicited" offer from someone who wants to do what you do. You must be able to prove your business's true value. It is not simply the number on a business valuation. Value maximization is much more than that, much more than tangible assets. It's your company's intangible asset value pertaining to your culture, clients, social perception, and structural innovation. These intangible assets will play a significant role in the potential buyer's decision and the proceeds received from the sale of your business! We create that transition strategy for your business before the exit, which will maximize value in all circumstances.

How can people find you, connect with you, and learn more?

—·· —————— ··—

Paul A. Kyrimis: Our website is www.LGStrat.com. You can also give me a call at 480-770-6115 or email Paul@LGStrat. com.

PAUL A. KYRIMIS, CEPA

FOUNDER
LEGACY GLOBAL STRATEGIES

Strategic, visionary, and collaborative professional with 20 years of experience in business strategy development, partnership management, and financial advisory strategies for strong personal and business outcomes. Guided by my core values of Intensity, Discipline, Perfect Effort, and Focus, surrounded by an Impenetrable Layer of Integrity, my purpose is to concentrate on others' success personally and professionally.

Results-oriented, with a strong background in developing and implementing innovative, forward-thinking solutions to some of the most challenging issues facing small business owners.

Engaging, collaborative leadership style, with an ease in translating highly complex strategies into actionable and aligned organizational objectives that drive success. Motivating, calm, executive-based presence with great strength in building high-performing teams and trust across the organization resulting in high growth and transformative business presence.

EMAIL:
Paul@LGStrat.com

PHONE:
480-770-6115

WEBSITE:
LGStrat.com

About the Publisher

Mark Imperial is a Best-Selling Author, Syndicated Business Columnist, Syndicated Radio Host, and internationally recognized Stage, Screen, and Radio Host of numerous business shows spotlighting leading experts, entrepreneurs, and business celebrities.

His passion is to discover noteworthy business owners, professionals, experts, and leaders who do great work and share their stories and secrets to their success with the world on his syndicated radio program titled "Remarkable Radio."

Mark is also the media marketing strategist and voice for some of the world's most famous brands. You can hear his voice over the airwaves weekly on Chicago radio and world-wide on iHeart Radio.

Mark is a Karate black belt; teaches Muay Thai and Kickboxing; loves Thai food, House Music, and his favorite TV shows are infomercials.

Learn more:

www.MarkImperial.com
www.BooksGrowBusiness.com